SPEED - READING PEOPLE

A step by step guide to understand how to analyze people. Learn body language secrets and the art of reading people.

BENEDICT SPOT
&
RICHARD EMPATH

TABLE OF CONTENTS

Chapter 1

HOW TO UNDERSTAND IN ADVANCE THE CHARACTER OF A PERSON

Research by MIT Media lab on negotiations conducted a study. In it, they found that, through careful study of a person's body language, and without a word of context, they came up with an exciting find. They were able to access with an 87% accuracy on the outcome of the negotiation, which they ran from telephone sales calls and business pitches.

Reading body language to understand in advance the character of a person and then know how to persuade them went beyond just looking at their body language as you communicate. In *The Silent Language of Leaders*, Carol Goman, a body language specialist, wrote about her research. In it, she identified ways in which we could accurately learn of another person's character. How they speak gives us a hint into their nature, and thus, knows how we could manipulate them.

Context: ignoring context if often one way in which we read body language wrong, for example, crossing hands if often seen as a sign being closed up. But, this can be inaccurate when the weather is cold.

Single reading: single reading was another way we made errors. Instead, Goman called for us to read body language in clusters. We needed to look beyond a single indicator to accurately judge a person's character and understand them in advance.

Baseline: here, you need to understand if a person always acted as they did when you or if they were acting out of character. A person acting out of style required you to be entirely keen on their other moves, as they could have hidden motives.

Blinding Your Biases: we all have biases and knowing them was vital in then reading people. Gorman said that liking/not liking a person, or whether or not we found them attractive, all affected us. Thus, knowing this was critical in helping you assess a person.

In another study, a personality psychologist at Texas University, Sam Gosling, stated that, unlike what we learned, first impressions were helpful to us. However, rather than sit on them as truths, we needed to update them. Thus, when you meet someone, take a moment. Trying to understand their intentions on the first meeting was useful, but you needed to be constantly monitoring the changes in their bodies. This understanding allows you to know how you will go about manipulating them to get what you wanted.

Sam went on to say that we needed to also pay attention to what he called identity claims. The identity claims said all we needed about what we wanted our goals, our attitudes, values, and many more. Therefore, someone wearing certain clothes, for example, would give you a peep into what message they wanted to pass. Again, to accurately gauge their character, and therefore, their intention, how they dressed and wore ornaments spoke of this. It was a statement that people used to display that they wanted others to know them, according to Sam.

Pennebaker, a researcher, also found that when telling the truth, most people tended to use 'I' a lot, while people lying would try to distance themselves by shying away from 'I,' as they were psychologically putting a distance between themselves and the lie. They also tended to avoid complicated language, as this would increase the likelihood of them stumbling and getting caught out on the lie.

But as we learned from the first study in this chapter, for a more accurate assessment, we need to cluster these signs. Various studies prove that it is possible to accurately read a person's body language and know their character if you do a close reading.

Chapter 2

BODY LANGUAGE; HOW IMPORTANT IS IT AND WHAT CAN WE LEARN?

Body language is a vital communication tool.

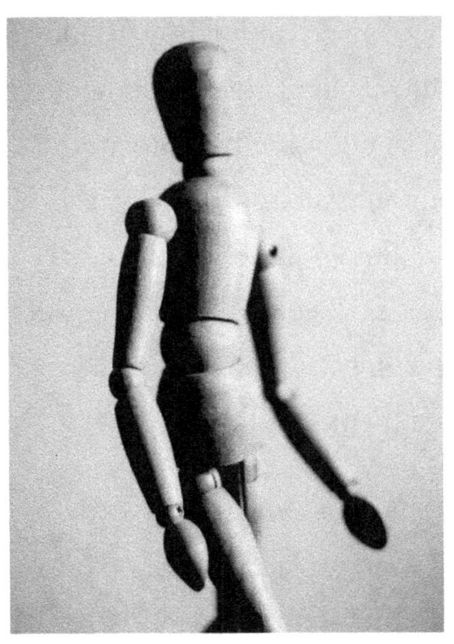

To accurately read a person, we need body language understanding. This reading allows us to look at intentions and their character, thus, you know how you will go about the interactions so that you get what you want. We touched on this revelation in the previous chapter, where researchers and psychologists let us in on the secrets that our bodies hold beyond our control.

While we can still control the movements that we were conscious of, there is still plenty that our bodies do that we cannot control. To understand this was to become better at reading body language and expertise interact with the person. Every action that we did during a conversation matters. No matter how innocuous it seemed, it let the other person a little deeper into who we were and what our intentions were. That, of course, as if they paid attention to these social cues themselves, and whether they understood the complexities of context and cluster reading, as well as being aware of how their biases affected them.

We transfer information through body language, and body language has two angles to it.

Decoding - decoding is your ability to interpret other people's body language. You need to decode their emotions, intention, and personality or character for their body language to have a meaning to you.

Encoding - this is how we control how we send signals to others. Encoding is what controls how we make first impressions and how we interact with others to get them to like us. To encode your messages for a better social impact, you need to know yourself well.

THE ROLE OF BODY LANGUAGE IN COMMUNICATION

Having looked briefly, at what body language entails, here, we look at the functions of body language. According to body language experts, body language is vital in communication in the following ways;

GIVING CUES

Regulating is where we use body language to keep the conversation going and ensuring that it is per social norms. In a social setting, there will often be indicators that we give and receive that gives us room to speak.

CONFLICTING/ WORD AND ACTION DO NOT MATCH.

Conflicting is when your body language is inconsistent with your words. You say you are comfortable and relaxed, but keep fidgeting with your phone, or keep shuffling your feet. Conflicting reveals what we may not be confident to express through words.

USING IT IN PLACE OF WORDS

You can substitute words with body language. Replacing is where we use body language in situations where we cannot talk. Substitution is especially useful to us when we are in public or want to keep our intentions hidden from another person within earshot.

GIVING MEAT TO WHAT WE SAY/ENHANCING

Complementing is where we use body language to add to what we are saying. We might gesture, for example, when we are talking about something passionately, or describing something that had an impact on us mentally. Complementing helps to strengthen what we are saying and lends credence to what we are saying. We will often use this to help the other party visualize what we are talking about. More often, we use it when we want or need to be descriptive.

GIVING DIRECTION

As with complementing, giving direction, or repeating, it also adds to what we are saying. However, unlike complementing, repeating is something that we do in basic conversation. You might say 'pass me the salt,' as you point to the salt shaker, for example. Repeating, rather than create emphasis as with complementing, acts as a direction to the person you are talking with.

While the above example makes it seem as though our body language operates in this bright cut patterns that we have described above, there are often overlaps. Context is also essential if we are to have an accurate assessment of another person's way of thinking. Thus, how we can use that to control them then to do what we want.

INFORMATION FROM BODY LANGUAGE

People's body language can lead us into their state of mental being. It also helps us gauge how they will respond to what we will tell them. Besides, it gives us clues to how they want us to think.

INTEREST

Standing close to or a distance away from someone can tell you a lot about whether someone likes or does not like you. Again, context is critical. Someone might stand close to you because there is little room to maneuver. Or they might stand further from you because they value their personal space or are introverted.

INTENTION

Someone mimicking how you move or using words that you use is someone that is trying to get you to trust and be comfortable around them. Take care of this as many cons use this move to get you to relax around.

You could use this move to help yourself relax around people if you want to become better at persuading them to see your point of view. However, let it flow and come naturally, as you will come off as creepy when you force it. This act then means that you need to take time to practice how to mimic effortlessly.

Someone who is flirting with you will also display certain traits. These traits will show you their sexual intentions. They include; a strong, yet delicate eye contact, or speaking in a lower-pitched voice. These are reliable indicators of physiological arousal.

CHARACTER/PERSONALITY

Body language provides us with a look into how a person's character is. A person who is sitting with an open posture, for example, might be a free, extroverted person.

Someone who is easily anxious and non-confrontational might have low self-esteem, for example. Someone maintaining steady eye contact might be trying to get your attention to misdirect you so that they may manipulate you.

Chapter 3

KNOW YOURSELF WELL
TO UNDERSTAND OTHERS

How well do you understand your body language? How well do you know of your reaction to factors, both internal and external?

Learning how to read another person's body language down to the finer details would be useless if you would not know how you come across yourself. Your attempt to persuade another person to your side would be inconsequential if you did not know how you are presenting yourself. You need to be aware of; the pitch of your voice, what are your arms saying, your eyes, and your facial expressions. Whatever you put out, is what determines how others pick up your message.

How to Know Yourself Better

IDENTIFY YOUR PERSONALITY

To be able to work on your general body posture, you first need to identify your personality. If you want to be more charismatic and are introverted, jumping right into trying to appear more outgoing might come off as you faking it. If you are extroverted and want to be charismatic, you need to know if you exude confidence or talk a lot.

Identifying your personality is critical as it gives you a gauge of what you desire and what you do not. If you are not very outgoing, then becoming outgoing just for the sake of it will work against you.

BODY POSTURE

Stand upright and try to be more relaxed if you are going to want to come off as confident and approachable. Unnatural slouched shoulders make you look less confident and unapproachable. When you speak to someone lean in a little to show that, you are interested in what they are saying. If you can help it, do not cross your arms. Let the other person get comfortable with you, and trust you.

BE FLEXIBLE WHEN COMMUNICATING

When you put a point across, and the other person does not seem to be receptive to the idea, learn how to change your body language. You could change the style of delivery to convince them to see your point of view too.

PRACTICE FACIAL EXPRESSION

Facial expression will often have a way of backing or taking away the punch from what we are saying. Practice this on the mirror in different scenarios. Look at how you express yourself when you are trying to convince, or when you are flirting, or when you are trying to be more confident. Refine them accordingly so that you have a better chance of convincing the other person of your point of view. Learning how to read others is an art, so is learning how to understand yourself. To read others better, you need to read yourself almost flawlessly.

INTENTION

Your intention guides how you align your body language to what you are saying. This book teaches you to persuade. Therefore, you need to learn how your body language will help you convince another person.

When speaking to someone else, for example, you can nod your head subtlety as you make your point. Take tab of their language and see how you can then use it to create a bond between the two of you so that they can grow to trust you.

GESTURES

Using gestures when you make a point makes you come off as more charismatic and thus, will make you more trustworthy. Make use of your arms when you make a point. Use it especially, to bring out your energy and emotions to the issue you are raising. Gestures make people grow more comfortable around you.

Once you understand the above, you will find that getting to manipulate and influence people becomes more manageable, since you use your knowledge of yourself to read them and act accordingly. You will read people well this way and analyze them with startling accuracy once you know yourself well.

Chapter 4

BODY LANGUAGE: BODY PARTS (THE MOVEMENTS AND POSTURES THAT TRANSMIT MESSAGES)

While we have touched on a few here and there, knowing how people communicate with various movements of their body parts will deliver a lot about them. You will decipher more about a person's personality and character, as well as their intention through how they move around. It includes how they move parts of their body around, and how they generally place themselves.

Body language has two major parts: Kinesics and proxemics. Kinesics is how someone moves their body or parts of their body. Proxemics, on the other hand, is the distance between bodies and what they signify. When you become a skilled observer, you will have a reasonably accurate glimpse into what someone is thinking. That way, you can then manipulate them better.

KINESICS

Kinesics refers to the movements of body parts, which someone can use to reinforce what they are saying, or can reveal what someone is trying to hide. This way, you gain an advantage that you can use to read their minds and make your move to persuade and influence them.

They include

BODY POSTURE - CLOSED/OPEN ARMS, SLUMPED SHOULDERS, ETC

Body posture is basically, how someone places their body. In body language, there are two types; closed and open body postures.

A closed body posture will typically mean that the person has his hands folded across his chest. They will cross their legs and face away from the person talking to them. Some people have slumped shoulders and curved backs.

This closed body posture often communicates either that the person is uncomfortable or not interested in what you are saying. When someone has slumped shoulders and a curved back, they may be struggling with confidence, or have a lot going through their mind and feel the weight weighing them down.

An open body posture, on the other hand, communicates interest and a desire to be approached and engaged. This posture will mean that the person is welcome to a conversation and will be receptive to your desire to speak with them.

When someone has an upright standing posture, they are likely more confident and happier. These people may be optimistic.

MIRRORING

Mirroring is the act where you match your body movements with the other person so that you create a synchronic situation that helps establish a bond between people. Mirroring, also called mimicry helps build trust, even when the person you are mirroring does not realize it.

While it sounds creepy, when you do it naturally, and with the right intention - to understand the other person better, it will help you read into what the other person is not saying.

Mirroring can take many forms. If the person you are talking to folds their arms, for example, it could be a sign that they are getting uncomfortable. However, you can copy them so that they become more at ease as they take it that they can trust you.

Alternatively, when they lean forward, it shows that they are interested in the conversation. Lean forward too. You could also lean forward as a cue for the other person to lean in. Leaning helps, you learn more about them to that, you can then read their mind and learn how you can persuade them.

You can mimick with words too. Take a keen interest in the words that the other person frequently. Then, begin to use them sparingly through the conversation.

Subconsciously, the other person will start to settle in your presence. This ease gives you room to analyze them and know how you can then approach them to persuade them of your point.

FACIAL EXPRESSIONS

Facial expressions are other very revealing body movements. Dr. Paul Ekman, a researcher, found that we use seven different micro-expressions that reveal the bigger picture; surprise, fear, disgust, anger, contempt, sadness, and happiness. These micro-expressions determined how to read well if someone was faking.

A genuine smile, for example, should involve various muscles on the face; cheeks, lips, and the eye muscles. A genuine smile will spread across the whole look. Keep note of that when someone smiles at you.

PROXEMICS

Proxemics is the study of how we relate to personal space. The thing with proxemics is that it is different from cultures and varies from individual to individual.

However, there is a little that we can learn from proxemics.

CLOSE DISTANCE - INTEREST

There is a close distance called the close range. We have this kind of distance with people that we are close with and trust. Often, entering into this distance with someone you are not close with is disturbing and creepy in many cultures and with many people.

So, to avoid turning off the other person, keep a safe distance. Ensure that you are close enough, but not too close to make them uncomfortable and closeout to your interactions.

Someone might also get close to you if they are interested in you. The person might not get too close to you, but they will get close enough to you to pass a message. If a person is trying to catch your attention, for example, they will get into your personal space but not get into the close distance. However, as we have learned, context is vital. Use this measure with other indicators, as someone might stand close to you because that is the appropriate distance in their culture, or that is just how they view space.

SOCIAL DISTANCE - IMPERSONAL/FORMAL

Social Distance is the distance we maintain with people such as business associates, people we are professional around. We often use social distance for coworkers who we are not well acquainted with or business associates.

The distance also refers to tilt. If one person sits in a position where they appear to look down on the other person, it may mean that they want to come across as authoritative.

PUBIC DISTANCE - RESPECTABILITY

This distance happens in a situation where you cannot get close to the other person because of the many limiting factors. At such a range, arm movement and gestures become critical. When in public, make a point of using head movement to pass your point, especially when you speak to a crowd. These body movements allow them to bond with you despite the distance. Look at some of the most admired public speakers. You will notice that they use hand movements and gestures a lot, as well as head movement and exaggerated facial expressions.

Our body language speaks in ways that we should take time to understand. But, as we have said, always use them in context for better analysis of the other person.

Chapter 5

BODY LANGUAGE IN MEN AND WOMEN – WHAT ARE ALL THOSE GESTURES THAT HIDE UNSPOKEN WORDS

Body language plays a significant role in our day-to-day communication. It refers to nonverbal gestures and signals that both men and women use to express emotions with their bodies without saying a word. Our body gestures and facial expression speak volumes about what we do not say when it comes to conveying information. Experts suggest that more than half of all communication is accounted for by our body language. Body language and learning how to interpret it is essential. While interpreting body language, it is vital to understand the context of the conversation and be attentive to any other cues. You should also not draw your conclusion by focusing on a single action, but you should look at signals as a group so that you can pull the right conclusion.

FACIAL EXPRESSIONS

The way we express our faces conveys a lot of information to others. You may say that you are well and good, but depending on the look on your face, some will be able to tell that you are not ok. People can trust or distrust what you are saying based on the look on your face

- **Happiness or approval** is usually indicated by a smile, while a frowning face will express sadness and disapproval.

- **A slight smile and a slight raise** of the eyebrows is a sign of being trustworthy, because it is a show of confidence and being friendly.

- **Intelligence** is associated with people who are joyful and have a smiling expression, more prominent noses, and narrower faces, rather than those with angry expressions.

THE EYES

The eyes are the windows to the soul because their movements can reveal the feelings and thoughts of a person during a conversation. Some things that you should look out for in the eyes are dilation of the pupil, blinking of the eyes, and whether a person averts their gaze or makes direct eye conduct.

- **Eye conduct** – if a person maintains direct eye conduct during a conversation, it shows that they are attentive and interested. However, a prolonged gaze is threatening and can be an attempt to control you. If a person frequently breaks wye conduct and keep on look away, it shows that they are uncomfortable, distracted, or trying to hide their real feeling and motives.

- **Blinking** – blinking should be natural. If a person blinks too rapidly that it is natural, it is a sign that they are uncomfortable or distressed. Someone may try to control their blinking intentionally to hide their true feelings purposely, so you should be careful to notice the infrequent blinking of the eyes. When blinking is accompanied by touching the mouth, eyes, and face, it is an indication that the person is lying.

- **Pupil size** – sometimes, emotions or feelings come with some changes in the size of the pupil. When the eyes are highly dilated, it is maybe an indication that someone is aroused or interested. It also shows a favorable response.

- **Looking down** –this indicates that the person is submissive or nervous.

- **Glancing** – it expresses a desire for something. Glancing at a person means that you desire to talk to them or be with them, while glancing at the door may indicate that the person wants to leave.

- **Looking upward and to the right** – it is a sign that someone is telling a lie. When people are trying to concoct a story using their imagination, they look that way.

- **Looking up and to the left** – it is a sign that the person is speaking the truth. People look that way when they are trying to recall an actual memory.

THE MOUTH

Someone who keeps can express insecurity, fear, or worry on chewing the bottom lip. Some may cover the mouth to cough or yawn politely, but it can also be a way of covering up a frown of expressing disapproval. You should watch out genuine smiles that show happiness, and false smiles meant to express cynicism or sarcasm. A genuine smile engages the whole face, while a false one is done with the mouth alone.

- **Pursed lips** – when a person tightens the lips, it is an indication of distrust, distaste or disapproval.

- **Biting the lip** - this is a sign of being stressed, worried, or anxious.

- Covering the mouth – a person may try to hide emotional reactions such as smirks or smiles by covering their mouths.

- **Turning the mouth up or down** - outright grimace, sadness or disapproval is expressed with the mouth slightly turned down. When the mouth is turned up slightly, it may be a show of feeling optimistic or happy.

- **A fake smile** – it uses the mouth only. It tries to show approval or pleasure, but it is a clear sign that the person is feeling otherwise.

- **A genuine smile** – it engages the whole face. It is an indication of happiness and approval and shows that the person is thoroughly enjoying your company.

- **Half-smile** – engages one side of the mouth, and it is used to express uncertainty, sarcasm, grimace, or cynicism.

ARMS AND LEGS

- **Crossed arms** – this might be a sign that someone is closed-off, defensive or self-protective.

- **Hands-on the hip** – when someone stands with their hands on the hip, it may show that they are in control or that they are ready. This can also be a sign of someone who is aggressive.

- **Hands clasped behind the back** – it is a sign that someone is feeling angry, anxious, or bored.

- **Fidgeting or tapping fingers rapidly** - is expresses frustration, impatience, or boredom.

- **Crossed legs** – indicates the need for privacy, dislike, discomfort or feeling closed-off

POSTURE

- **Open posture** – the trunk of the body is kept exposed and accessible, and it shows willingness, friendliness, and being free with others.

- **Closed posture** – the legs and the harms are kept crossed, and the body trunk is often hidden by the person hunching forward. It shows that someone is being anxious, unfriendly and hostile.

PROXIMITY

The distance a person keeps from you during a conversation speaks volumes.

- **Standing or sitting close** – it is a good sign of rapport. It shows that the other person views you favorably. However, if a person steps into your personal space and begins to touch you, it shows that they are trying to control you.

- **Backing up or moving away** - when you move closer and the other person steps backward it is an indicator that there is no mutual connection.

Chapter 6

PERSONALITY TYPES – HOW TO INTERPRET THEM

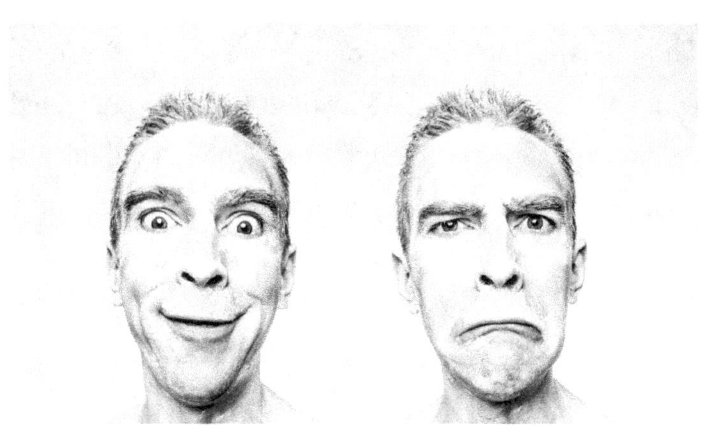

When you interact with a person for a while, you can interpret and tell the type of personality they are. Personality type refers to the different types of individuals as have been classified through psychology based on the way they tend to behave, feel, and think. Personality is what makes a person who they are, and each person has an idea of their personality type. Some people are thick-skinned, others are sensitive, and others are bubbly while others are reserved.

Several ways have been put forward to measure personality, but mostly, psychologists focus on personality traits. The Big Five has come to be the most widely accepted of these traits. It is also called the FFM standing for the five-factor model or the OCEAN.

These five factors are the ones expressed by the acronym CANOE or OCEAN. These factors are affected by how someone was brought up. Genetics and the environment affect these personality traits almost equally. Let us dive in and analyze each of these five broad types of personalities and the attributes associated with each one of them so that you can know to interpret them.

EXTRAVERSION

This is the widely recognized personality type. It is common for you to hear people say that someone is either an extrovert or an introvert. This personality type is based on someone having a lot of interaction with the external world. Extraverts are known to be a kind of social butterflies and drive pleasure from interactions with others and are often known to be full of energy. They are lively, sociable, and chatty, and they draw power and energy from their interactions with crowds. They are action-oriented persons and tend to be enthusiastic. They are assertive and talkative and have high group visibility .they may dominance in social settings.

On the other hand, introverts have lower energy and are less involved with the social world. They have lower engagement with the social world and deliberately tend to be low-key and quiet. This should not be confused with being shy or depressed, but being more independent of their social world. Being shy refers to the fear of social situations and interactions or being unable to function socially, but an introvert can be charming at parties and come-together events with colleagues. They like to have their time alone and require less social stimulation, not because they are antisocial or unfriendly, but because they are reserved in social events. They just prefer being solo or in small-group activities.

AGREEABLENESS

Individuals with this personality have a general concern for social harmony. People with agreeable personality place premium value in getting along well with others, and they have the willingness to consider other people even if it means sacrificing self-interests. They are associated with kindness, being helpful, generosity, and being trusting and trustworthy. They are optimistic about their look of humanity.

On the other hand, disagreeable individuals put their self-interest first at the expense of good relations with others. They have less concern about other peoples' wellbeing and will rarely reach out for others. They tend not to be friendly or cooperative because they are skeptical and suspicious of others. They are seen as being argumentative, challenging, competitive, or untrustworthy people.

OPENNESS

People with this type of personality are open to the experience. They have a general appreciation for adventure, art, imagination, unusual ideas, emotion, and other experiences. They are open to the excitement, have intellectual curiosity, sensitive to beauty, and are always ready to experiment with new things. They have a good understanding of their feelings and are associated with creativity. Scoring high on openness may be taken to mean that they are hard to predict, can hold unconventional beliefs, may lack focus, and indulge in risky behavior such as taking drugs. Individuals in this category seek to actualize themselves through euphoric and intense experiences.

Conversely, people with low openness are pragmatic and data-driven, and seek to gain fulfillment through endurance. They are seen to have closed minds and are perceived to be dogmatic. They are better off sticking to their habits, avoid adventurous activities, and tend not to like new experiences.

NEUROTICISM

Individuals in this category tend to experience negative emotions. These emotions include depression, anger, or anxiety. It is associated with emotional instability and connected to low tolerance for stress or aversive stimuli. Scoring high in neuroticism scales means that the individual is emotionally reactive and susceptible to stress. They tend towards being loose and disrespectful in the way they express their emotions. They make a mountain out of small issues. More likely, they may misinterpret an ordinary situation and see it as a threat. It becomes hopelessly tricky for them when they encounter minor frustrations.

Neuroticism is interlinked with a defeatist attitude and being pessimistic towards work, apparent anxiety towards work, and the confidence that work hinders personal relationships. Scoring high in neuroticism is connected with a high possibility to show skin-conductance reactivity, with diminished ability to regulate emotions which affects one's capability to think with clarity, make sound choices and deal with stress effectively. People who score high in neuroticism lack contentment with their achievements in life and have a high chance of falling into clinical depression. They tent to go through more negative life events; their psychological wellbeing is worse off.

On the other hand, those scoring less on neuroticism are hardly annoyed and have less emotional reactivity.

They are usually calm and have emotional stability. They do not experience persistent negative feelings.

CONSCIENTIOUSNESS

This personality type is marked with the ability to show self-discipline. Individuals in this category have a strong sense of duty and strive to achieve without paying much attention to external expectations or measures. They are excellent planners, focused on achievement, dependable, and disciplined. They understand how to regulate, control, and give direction to their impulses. Stubbornness and focus are associated with high conscientiousness.

Low conscientiousness is perceived as being flexible, freewheeling, and spontaneous, but sometimes it can appear as a lack of reliability and sloppiness and may tend to be careless. It is a helpful personality trait and has been connected to better achievement in school and the workplace.

With such knowledge, you can interact with a person for a while, interpret, and tell the type of personality they have.

Chapter 7

HOW TO DECIPHER VERBAL COMMUNICATION

To fully understand and decode the message in the other person's words, there are some things about verbal communication that you should master. This is regardless of whether you are engaging in face-to-face or written communication.

BE AN ACTIVE LISTENER

To master the art of active listening, you must be able to listen beyond the words being spoken. This means that you listen, aiming to decipher and understand the message being communicated. A lot of people listen with the wrong motive and end up missing what the other person is saying. Instead of listening to decipher the other person's point of view, they listen while thinking about how they will respond. They fail to concentrate on what the speaker is saying and miss the point.

When you listen carefully and actively, you can answer thoughtfully, taking into account the other person's perceptions, views, and opinions. The rule of thumb should always be to listen more and talk less. But how do you become an active listener? Here is how:

1. Pay attention

You should learn to give others full attention when they are speaking:

- Maintain eye contact by looking at the speaker directly while they share their side of the story.

- While the other person is talking, don't try to think about how you will reply or respond.
- Pay attention to the speaker's body language and interpret it
- Avoid any distraction by anything else that is going on around you

2. Show your interest in what the other person is saying.

- Encourage the speaker by nodding your head and using other prompts like "yep," "uh-huh," and so on.
- Highlight your engagement using your body language, such as maintaining an open posture, nodding your heads, and smiling.

3. Clarify your understanding

Clarify how you have understood the speaker's message with them. As you do that, keep your beliefs and judgments out of the way.

- Paraphrase and summarize as a way of reflecting on what you have heard. Do this periodically as the conversation goes on to help you understand better. It is also a great way to help the other person feel that you are listening. For example, "if I got you clearly, you said that …." Or "correct me if I'm wrong, but my understanding of that is …"

- Ask non-judgmental questions to seek clarification and ensure that you grasp everything.
- When you are not sure of what the speaker says or means, admit.
- If it will help, ask the person to repeat what they said
- Ask for elaborative examples
- Accept to be corrected in the event where you get what the speaker said wrongly.

4. Don't redirect or interrupt the conversation

When you interrupt another person's speech, you reduce your time for understanding the message, besides irritating the speaker.

- Do not interject unnecessarily, when the other person is speaking. Let them finish their part, and don't say anything unless the speaker has driven home the point they are trying to make.
- Don't go outside the topic or try to divert the conversation based on your beliefs, views, or opinions.

5. Provide a suitable response

- When you make a response, try to be honest. Don't attack or make the other person feel bad. Doing so is immature and unhelpful.
- If you want to give your views, perceptions, or opinions, do so in a polite manner.

6. Avoid the common enemies of active listening. They include:

- Arguing
- False assumptions which come as a result of jumping into conclusion
- Losing concentration
- Trying to quickly formulate a response before the other person finishes making their point.

BE EMPATHETIC

This means that you can understand and identify with other person's emotions by imaging yourself in their shoes or positions. When you have the ability to know how others feel, it can help you understand them when they communicate. You will also be able to convey your ideas and thoughts sensibly and care for other peoples' feelings.

If you want to understand other people's verbal communication, take these concrete steps to develop empathy.

- Put yourself in the other person's position. Think of the time when you experienced the same feelings/ emotions which the speaker is experiencing. It doesn't have to be precisely the same, but you can think of a related situation.

- Think of how you would feel if someone keeps on interrupting you before you make your point. That way, you will learn to let others talk without interrupting them.

- Observe your colleagues well as they speak and try to grasp the feelings or emotions they are communicating through the words.

- If you notice that your colleague is conversing emotionally, do not despise or ignore them. Understand it and address it. Give them time to cool down.

- Seek to understand, but not to judge. For instance, when your colleague seems disinterested and cold at first, you may capture a feeling of being annoyed with them. But after you learn that they have a problem of being socially anxious, you will be more sympathetic and give them time to relax and make their point.

- Don't seek to corner your colleague, or engage yourself in a conversation with the mentality of winning it. Learn to regulate your voice so that you can communicate your empathy by being sincere and keeping your body language open.

SEEK TO UNDERSTAND FIRST

If you want the other person to understand you, seek to understand them first. Don't try to force your ideas, thoughts, perceptions, or opinions on others. To do that is to approach a conversation with a closed mind, and it will only result in unnecessary arguments. The best way to decipher verbal communication is to listen and understand the beliefs, thoughts, and perspectives of the other person so that you can know why they hold them. You do not have to agree with them, but at least you will understand why they think the way they think.

Therefore, learning to listen actively, being empathetic, and mastering the art of understanding others first, is the master key to deciphering any form of verbal communication. Running into conclusions will only result in assumptions and confusion, and you will end up missing the point the other person is attempting to make.

Chapter 8

THE MEANING OF THE WORDS

Words are an expression of an individual's thoughts and emotions. No matter how much someone tries to hide what is in their mind, their words will always betray them in one way or another. The world of dark psychology employs this technique to get into people's minds and perform wonders. When it comes to the meaning of words, dark psychology does not pay attention to the literal meaning of those words; it is never related to meanings found in the dictionary. What someone will look for is the actual meaning coming from within the speaker; what is really in their mind. The following combination of factors will help you decipher the actual meaning in the words of the target.

PITCH

This is the pitch in the speaker's speech. Do they say some words with a high voice and others with a low one? The tone with which words are said speaks volumes about the feelings and thoughts of an individual. Let us look at the following example; a politician and presenter are having a chat on national television.

POLITICIAN: the citizens must be excited that I am selling my manifestos here today.

PRESENTER: oh yeah? It is expected.

POLITICIAN: My social media is flooding with messages of goodwill (low); my opponents must see that (high).

PRESENTER: but first let us hear what you have in store for the people.

POLITICIAN: most of them already know my agendas, but I will repeat it anyway.

PRESENTER: You cannot be so sure, sir. It is your first time on-air; this is a good opportunity to boost your popularity (low).

POLITICIAN: (whispering) very well, I did not know I am not known.

PRESENTER: hey, just not enough (low).

(The politician sighs)

From this dialogue, we see that the politician is trying hard to make the presenter believe that he is popular while he is not. He cunningly tries to avoid addressing the issues directly by using general words like 'agendas' and 'manifestos'. He manipulates his way into the pre-senter's mind and finds the truth-he is not all that pop-ular. The use of the words 'citizens' 'the people' and 'social media' indicate that the politician is targeting popularity. We can also get to read the politician's mind from the pitch in his voice. He says his social media pages are flooding with messages of goodwill with a low voice, an indication that he desperately needs the fame he is talking about. The low voice means the 'flooding' is a mere exaggeration. The second part of that statement is more of a threat directed at his opponents, some sort of propaganda, 'my opponents must see'. The use of the word 'must' about his opponents tells us that he is just bluffing. He has no control over what his opponents should or should not do whatsoever.

PICK CUES

Sometimes the speaker does not bring out their thoughts using the right words. They will use a variety of synonyms and other techniques to deliberately mislead the listener. Dark psychologists will pick these cues from the words spoken and use them to accurately read the speaker's mind. Let us look at the following examples.

"After the wedding, I patiently waited in the queue until I got served."

The clue here is the word 'patiently'. This statement means the speaker was not only hungry but they also had no alternative other than following the long queue to the end. It says a lot about their financial position as well as the significance of that event to them. This information can be used to press the right buttons if the person is to be manipulated into doing something they would otherwise not agree to easily. You could promise such a person plenty of food or financial assistance as a way of winning them. Here is another practical example:

"Not that I'm afraid of heights, I just don't trust our engineers."

These are the words of someone that is afraid of heights but finds a good excuse to cover it up. The mention of the word 'afraid' is enough evidence of the underlying fear. This fact is reinforced by the kind of reason they give. Technically, all buildings have not been built by one person and unless it is condemned, then there is no cause for alarm. And does it mean the person will never enter a high-story building? Not, the bottom line here is the person is afraid of heights. You can easily use this weakness on their part to manipulate them.

The trick when it comes to picking cues is no analyzing every word spoken by someone in a sentence. Relate every word with the previous and subsequent one to get its meaning and context. This will help you to identify misplaced words that will serve as cues. The cues will, in turn, put you in a better position to read someone's mind quite easily.

LOOK OUT FOR REPETITIONS

Words that are repeated repeatedly are something to pay attention to if you are looking to discover what is in someone's mind. It means the speaker is desperately trying to communicate their thoughts but they do so in a way that people will not understand. These words can be synonyms or related sentiments so it takes a lot of scrutinizes to identify. Look at the following three statements.

I would love to have a big car when I find a good job.

My mum would have bought an expensive dress if my neighbor's daughter's graduation was mine.

I watched an action movie with robots that built castles in the sky.

The three sentences have a consistent similarity in that they are centered on big things, luxurious ones for that matter. These things are the person's biggest fantasies. If you analyze the sentences keenly, you will notice that the words 'big', 'expensive', and 'sky' are related. They all have something to do with success. This tells us that the speaker has a strong desire to live largely. It also tells us that their current condition is nowhere near their fantasies. This intense craving for material success can be used to manipulate such an individual. Dark psychologists would listen to someone speak, not to understand them but to notice those words that person keeps emphasizing.

Chapter 9

HOW TO PAY ATTENTION TO DETAILS

To effectively hack someone's mind, you must learn to pay attention to every single detail concerning every single word they utter and body movements. The words they use are major cues people use to express their thoughts. Body movements are just mere reinforcements for those words. Try to create a connection between every word spoken and the accompanying movement, these two could be simultaneous or separate. Learning to relate words and movements will come in handy when looking out for people that want to manipulate you. We shall study single words and movements in this chapter as a technique of paying attention to details. This will be illustrative for ease of understanding.

THE LINK BETWEEN BODY MOVEMENT AND WORDS

Prominent public speakers undergo intense training before standing before an audience to speak. Those close to figures like presidents and religious leaders will confirm to you that indeed the training can last several months or even years. The reason this happens is to ensure whatever they speak to the audience is exactly what is in their mind, whether it is the truth or just lies. However, one can still read their minds accurately despite vigorous training. The relationship between words and movements can easily sell them out; it is difficult to fake emotions throughout the speech. If someone is narrating a sad event, for example, their movements will be quite different from those associated with an exciting event. Let us analyze the following case.

"Ladies and gentlemen, we are saddened beyond the comprehension of words by the sudden and untimely demise of our brothers and sisters in the ferry that sank on Monday morning. Our gallant men in blue have been working day and night to retrieve the bodies since the tragedy happened. Unfortunately, it breaks my heart to announce to you that all has been an effort in futility. Our intelligence has revealed that the bodies have been buried deep in the murky seawaters, a situation that is complicating the process of retrieving the bodies, as we do not have sufficient equipment for such an undertaking. We require more than four tanks of oxygen for each diver; a resource that is not plenty in supply at the moment. We have also come to a logical conclusion that sending those divers to the bottom of the ocean is nothing short of putting their innocent lives at great risk. We have therefore decided to call off the operation to avoid losing more lives. I know this is not the best news for the families of the victims but it is the right thing to do. We shall hold a vigil for the victims by the sea for the next two days. It is not enough but it is the best we can do at this point, our hands are tied."

Let us analyze this speech by a government official about an ill-fated sunken ferry that claimed the lives of all its occupants. We want to try and read the speaker's mind and verify these claims. We shall be in a position to tell whether this is just another ploy to cover up for the government's unwillingness to find the remains of its deceased citizens or there is some logic in it.

"WE ARE SADDENED"

We know whether this statement is genuine by observing the way the speaker says it and accompanying movements. First of all, the word 'saddened' should be mentioned with a low, dejected and troubled voice. Second, it should be accompanied by a little bow or dilation of the pupils. To emphasize it further, there ought to be a brief silence before the speaker continues.

"BEYOND THE COMPREHENSION OF WORDS"

This statement means that words cannot explain the feeling, so actions ought to play that role. The speaker could press their lips together or cross their arms to show despair.

"BROTHERS AND SISTERS"

The look in the face of the speaker as these words come out of mouth should reveal the feeling one would have when talking about the loss of a real brother and sister. Mentioning those words would likely send shivers all over the speaker's body. The lips could tremble, the voice ought to be shaky and they could even choke in their words. If the voice is smooth and clear, then we have reason to doubt the speaker's true feelings about the victims.

"EFFORT IN FUTILITY"

This statement implies despair. The speaker's voice should express that, especially when saying the word 'futility'. Body movements that could be associated with this statement include crossing arms, slight bowing of the head and bringing feet together.

"MURKY"

The literal meaning of this word is dark and gloomy. Regarding ocean waters, it becomes even scarier. We should pay attention to the way the speaker says this dreadful word. We expect his face to show this by looking just like it-dark and gloomy. We need to feel the pain of saying the word in his voice; is it shaky? We need to see the pain written on his face. His hands should also speak of the feeling. Are the fists clutched? Are the fingers crossed? Are the arms folded around the chest? Look for anything that will show the dreadful nature of that word.

"LOGICAL CONCLUSION"

The way the speaker says the word 'logical' should tell you whether the conclusion is indeed a logical one or it is just another wild claim. The amount of stress applied to the word indicates the extent of seriousness. If he says it casually, then it means he is just trying to dupe his listeners with a technical word. Also, does his explanation support the weight of the word? Is it logical that a whole country is unable to acquire enough oxygen for the exercise?

By keenly analyzing some single words used by the speaker, together with his body movements, we will be able to read his mind and ascertain the sincerity of his words. If the speaker had the intention of manipulating this audience, only those equipped with mind-reading skills will escape the snare.

Chapter 10

LIES (LIKE DISCOVERING A LIE, THE BEST TECHNIQUE TO UNDERSTAND A LIE FROM MOVEMENTS OF WORDS, OR IN BEHAVIOR)

Remember that time you did something without the permission of your parents. How did you feel when lying? Probably you felt unsure whether you will succeed in cheating your parents. But how do your mother or father notice that you were lying? Perhaps it is your behavior or the choice of words you undertook. Many situations force omen to rest, but one should know deceitful conduct is a vice. It will still cause chaos among your loved ones. You may succeed in lying to the court of something you had done, but that guilt and conscience will not leave you. Therefore you must be pure always like where the truth will set you free.

One aspect to check is the physical body movement. Remember that everyone experiences some uneasiness when cheating; thus, the body will tend to detach itself from that deceitful mood. These moods can be dissipated in very many ways that change your behavior. That is where some people shake and mumble when they are telling a lie. That cheating guilt will envelop them and make them shiver with the fear of being caught lying. Moreover, if you spot a whitish element in the lips, know that they are lying.

Check on their eyes. Remember that the eyes will read your heart and mind and dispel information according to your emotional state. Therefore when you lie, then there are some signs showed by the eyes. Those who blinks a lot of time while telling a story is evidence of cheating. Your eyeballs may know if you are cheating too. Sometimes your eyes may dance around your sockets when you are deceiving someone. It is like that guilt triggers to move around the sockets

Consider other body reactions to spot in a liar. These different reactions are fidgeting methods. They are objects one holds to try to hide or escape from the cheating mood. That is where some people feel nervous and look uncomfortable at your presence. Some may like to maintain a long-distance from you because they suspect if they are near, you can easily read their lies. Others would decide to play with the items available like trying to tighten a dress, touching your hair or any other piece of clothing.

Look at their change in their tone. That means the tonal variation is very significant to detect the lies. For example, you can quickly identify this change of voice of a person in normal circumstances. You will undoubtedly realize that change. Maybe in their stable mind, they talk slowly and tranquil, but at this time they speak fast and stammers. They also have an inconsistent tone, where it changes at any time. That is because they are describing imaginative events where they forget the right voice balancing.

Diagnose their chat manner when intermingling with other people. Liars would take time to think of words to fill in making a story amusing. That means that their word flow is unfortunate as they take a long time to make a sentence. You will realize how they use jargon and vocabulary to deviate your interest in what you want them to tell you. Moreover, they can chatter to make the words look meaningless, which would make you lose attention in them.

Deceivers always talk in general terms. They avoid the use of the first pronoun persona but use the general pronouns like 'they', 'them', 'him' or others. That is a way of trying to cover their involvement in that ordeal. They may even distract you with exciting news which is different from your earlier discussion. That is like trying to talk about the current crisis, politico, sports and other fascinating subjects.

Identify their inconsistency in their communication. That is one strategy used in the prisoners' dilemmas. If you are telling the truth, then you should respond to the same answer even when asked later. However ask liars the same thing they said earlier, and you will realize how they forget that sateen. Moreover, you will know how they struggle to revert thee words they said.

Their facial communication is another way that can tell you whether they are dishonest. Cheaters always show different visual expressions. That is where if these respondents are gloomy and bored if you keep investigating their honesty Others will be excited if they feel you have fallen for their trap. They still fake a moaning face to harness your sympathy. Check on their eye contact to know how they look at you. If they watch you with nervous or looks you with an uncertain attitude, see that they are lying. Moreover, they will dodge your eye contact as they feel guilty of lying.

All of their behaviors are exaggerated. Look at their smiles which they fake. Remember that smiles convey honesty, sincerity, and understanding. Real smiles typically appear naturally contracted on your muscles. However, fake smiles are consciously contracted and appear elongated on the cheeks than the genuine smiles. Look at the laughter, it is overdone, and it goes over more minutes than usual. If you are asking them maybe about reported stolen cash from a bank account which they were involved in, you will rely on their exaggerated pity. Their eyes will look you with mercy, such that you can forgive them if they are caught. Contemplate how an innocent person is usually bold and confident about what they are saying.

Pay attention to how they voice the word "No." It is a means of opposing any issue on liars. They will say no even a situation where not requiring their response. They will always jump to conclusions like "are you implicating me, do you think am the thief "? Normally, truthful people, that idea of the thief will not come to their mind as quickly as those of the guilty one. Look at where they focus their eyes when saying "no." You will realize that either they will close their eyes, look in a different direction or say it after hesitating for sometimes. Their tone in saying "no "will also appear exaggerated.

Chapter 11

TRUTH (HOW TO RECOGNIZE A FACT)

Honesty is the significant parameter and virtue that is recommendable. That is particularly even in the jobs and occupations where one is required to curb the corruption cases. There are times when one is needed to tell the truth. For example, in the court, you will mostly hear the judge or the jury demanding to know the truth. Truthfulness is a virtue that must be prominent in you everywhere you go. Most of the time, you will find yourself in a situation where the truth will set you free. Imagine that you are captured and tortured in a military war. What proximity of the pin would make you tell the truth? Therefore if you can be honest at least, there will be no needles been inserted in your fingertips.

Ways to Know Someone Is Telling the Truth.

Check on the facial expression when the person is telling a story. They usually will show a confident face. Can you differentiate that person who is shy and sure, one aspect you can look in both of them is their face? They know what they are saying is true and will want you to show it even with their face. In every mood of the story, they will express every feeling. In every narration, there is a mixed reaction. There is that point in the story where it was joyous, and then the situation changed when there were terrible outcomes. Therefore the narrator will express all the moods with the facial manifestation. If it were a liar involved, he or she would forget to input the necessary expression on the face.

Look at how they express their point of the statement. The honest speak with clarity and are precise. There is no space for ambiguity as those characters explain all details perfectly. Their words seem to flow well as they are describing how a situation transpired. If they were lying, then you ought to note some hesitation in their statements. That is where they are looking for the word to fill the puzzle. There is no exaggeration, but they speak on a real basis. The tone used in that point is consistent. That would be unlikely for anyone who is lying as they would stress the major points they want to be heard and lower the tone on their unwanted details.

Recognize how steady their breath is. The falsifiers tend to cheat and will feel guilty of the wrong they are saying. That guilt is dissipated with their breathing problems. You can know even when they are panicking as they breathe inconsistently. They may start transpiring slowly than that rhythm changes and you realties how they began much breathing fast. A genuine person will breathe consistently at the same rhythm when they thought the conversation person will still look at you at some points. If the individual fails to see you or maintain much eye contact, know that they are lying.

The truth is something that you own and should not be deviated; however, many times, you are asked of a story. Look at the techniques most investigators use, which is the prisoners' dilemma. That is where the suspects are locked in different rooms. Each culprit is also told to narrate their side of the story. What will most detectives look like the divergence and the correction of the story? If the suspects seem to contradict, then one of them lying. If they say the same thing, then they are hones, or they had planned a lie. It is upon you, the detective to use all the instruments sat your disposal to ensure that the information being said is true. Their knowledge is still consistent as they do not deviate even if asked five or ten years to come. There is no way you can forget an event, but you can remember what you said earlier. If then you are lying, you will contradict your earlier spoken words.

Speaking in completes sentence is what define you an honest guy, liars will try to make their statement a puzzle that you may find hard understanding. Reliable individuals will speak in long sentences with clarity. You will not find any ambiguity in the report. What you will identify in their phrases is the completeness of the sentence structure. You will not find any jargon and vocabulary in their comments.

Trust in your instincts when inquiring for information. These are the inner conscience that makes you sensitize something. If you feel something terrible will happens, then it might occur, which is a result of your instincts. It is like the first impression that you will generate from a person. If you feel that this person is telling the truth, then they must be accurate, but if you think otherwise take caution.

The body motions of these people are other determinates. Remember that when you are honest, you are very confident. Therefore you do not expect to see somebody covering their mouth, head, chest or throat to be truthful. The posture of your body will also tell if you are bending one side and sitting with closed legs as if you are hiding something important. Some may prefer a far distance from you as they feel insecure about your presence. Their cheating nature makes them feel vulnerable to stay close to you.

Honesties do not like blaming others for their mistakes. They will, however, blame themselves. They are ready to face the consequences and feel that they are responsible for a disdainful act. They trust their inner feelings which they know may result in the wrong actions taken. Contrary to them, there are the cons and the fraudsters who like blaming others on their misfortunes they do not want to be caught as they fear the penalties. Note how those persons drag somebody else name in the story. Identify how also they will try to justify themselves.

Perhaps you have taken an oath or a vow on a wedding aisle. How did you feel when you made some unconditional promises? You must have felt happy and pressured not to break any promise. If you want an honest individual note how they swear before narrating the ordeal. Yes, the cheaters will also declare, but the guilt will be drawn on their faces; however much they hate. People reeling the truth usually like swearing as they stress their integrity.

Chapter 12

TECHNIQUES AND PRACTICAL METHODS TO ACTIVELY ANALYZE PEOPLE

For you to understand the personality of a person, you need to examine them. You need to dig deep into their life so that you can know the kind of person you are dealing with. For you to understand how to treat them, you need to go the extra mile. You need to know how you can provoke them and whether they are hostile when they are subject to certain situations. You need to be in a position that you can tell what is happening when you look at them. The way they communicate should say to you more about them. That is the reason you should pay attention to everything that is happening in their life. When you analyze someone, you will get to know what they like and what they dislike. There are numerous ways that you need to consider that will help you to analyze a person. They include and not limited to;

HOW TO ASK THE RIGHT QUESTIONS

When you need to ask the right question, it means that you need a clear answer from someone. You have to be discreet so that you will avoid a lot of complications. When you complicate things, you will not get the right information that you require from someone. That means that if you do not get the correct information, you will not understand them. Meaning you will not achieve your goal, which is to analyze them. Avoid rhetorical questions because that will not make you get the answer that you need. It might piss off the person, and they fail to let their guard down. Asking a rhetorical question means that you are forcing them to give you a specific answer that you need. The answer may be different from what you need to know. But because you have forced them to say that they will say it to please you. That will get you nowhere since you designed the answer you need and it may not be the real thing. When you are asking the question, make sure you do that in a friendly way. Rightly asking a query will not make the person defensive, and they will be comfortable to answer any question. When you demean a person, they will not be satisfied to give you honest feedback.

If you need to know someone better, do not try to set traps for them making them be on the spot. Ask a question without erecting a box around the person for them to be free to answer you. That is how you can know the kind of person you are dealing with. It will be appropriate to make an open-ended question so that the person you want to analyze will have the freedom to explain more about it. When you do not place bonds, you will give a person the time to respond appropriately in detail as well as nuance. Giving them a chance to make their choices will cause them to pour out their hearts to you. Even if you are up to something, you must avoid being direct so that the respondent will not be rigid. As you are asking the questions, you need to be as well willing to listen. Take a breather at times so that the person will not think as though you are interrogating them and refuse to give you the answers. They will not be quick to know that you are on a fact-finding mission. If you ask a question and you sense that they are uncomfortable, it is good that you rephrase it. You must be grateful when the person agrees to answer the questions so that they can feel appreciated.

WHEN TO BE AGGRESSIVE

When things are tough to be a bit aggressive so that you will get the information that you need. Do that knowing that you are after your interest and you need to make the person talk. Although you will be aggressive, you need to make sure that you do your research on the person thoroughly. You need to do that politely so that the person will not get pissed off. When they are annoyed, they will not let you access anything about you, and it will get harder on you. Someone may even turn to be a stranger, and they were a friend before you got aggressive. That is the reason you should do it in the politest way possible. Give them enough space so that they will pour out all that you require to know about them. Talking too fast will make them hold some information that you may be necessary. Do not brag since that will make them think that you are not of the same level and they will not be open to you.

WHEN TO OBSERVE THE BEHAVIOR OF OTHERS

Put in mind that people behave in different ways, and each is unique. When you see the behavior of a person, you will learn more about them. Their actions will speak more about the person they are. When one is thinking that, no one is seeing them that is the time that they will be the real person they are. You need to time that moment that the person thinks they are alone and you can see the person they are. Check their habits and know what differentiates them from other people. From each observation that you are likely to make, you will have a brief thing to learn about the person. When you are figuring out the views that you have made, it is necessary that you establish whether that is the real thing. At times, you can make a conclusion that is not right, and that will give you the wrong image of the person. If you are illegal in the end that you are making, you need to improve your observation techniques so that you will not misjudge things. When you create an observation, it is time that you use your imagination to think about how that person is like. That will give you an analysis of the person they are and what is unique in them that you cannot find on anyone else.

Chapter 13

HOW TO TAKE ADVANTAGE OF THE TECHNIQUES LEARNED TO ACHIEVE SUCCESS AND ENJOY THE ESTEEM OF OTHERS

You need to know that the methods you are using can make you successful in analyzing someone and can as well earn you respect. That is what you should aim for when you embark on the journey to investigate someone. You need to gain their esteem even though you are out on a mission. That is the reason they should not know that you are up to something. When they come to a realization that you are researching on them, they will not be comfortable with you, and they might end up disrespecting you. Be polite when you are asking the questions you have to, and you will hit your goal. When you get your target that is the moment that you will know that, you are a success. When you get, the full information that you need about the person is when you need to rest.

Here is how you need to take advantage of the techniques that you decide to put in place to analyze a person.

KNOWING YOURSELF

When you are set on the journey to see the person you are, you will have access to your hidden wisdom. That will be so because you will behave enough space as well as time to explore that person you are. Knowing yourself better will then give you the chance to analyze the person next to you. You will explore new opportunities that you were not aware of them before. That will make you achieve great things since you are now aware of your potential. When you get to know the real person you are, you will with no doubt, be productive and with fewer efforts. You will be more inspired to do great things without having to invest much power. When you know who you are, it will be easy for you to make decisions, and you will not have to struggle to make the decision that fits you. In that way, you will attract respect from the people around you since you are a self-driven person. When you know what you want as well as who you are, that is the time that you will begin being successful and doing great things.

TRUTH

When you always tell the truth, it will set you free, and you do not have to remember anything you said so that you do not mess up. Once you tell a lie, you have to keep reminding it in case you are asked the same thing, and you will not contradict yourself. When you learn to speak the truth, you will with no doubt earn trust as well as respect. You will gain respect for who you are and will like to be associated with you. When you learn to tell lies, most are the times that you will fail since you will prefer to use the wrong channels of doing things. The truth will always make you win the trust of people, and you will have more connections through that. You need to know that for you to be successful, you need people to elevate you. No one will be willing to be there for you if all you can do is lie to them. When you are truthful, you will be trusted. It means that everyone will offer you an opportunity to use your potential to the benefit of all. You will be more confident, and you will not even lie to yourself, which is a good recipe for a person's downfall. You will not be betraying your thoughts as well as beliefs, and that will earn you respect from people. Telling the truth will attract people who are truthful as well.

INTERPRETING PERSONALITY

When you want to analyze someone, you need to explain their character so that you will know who they are. In the process, you will as well see the person you are and your preferences. When you are aware of your preferences, you will be efficient as well as productive. You will know when you are beyond your boundaries, and that will help and the extent you can go. When you are aware of that, you will improve in terms of productivity, efficiency as well as time management. When all that is in combination, there is no room for negotiations, and you will be successful in the end. When you know your personality, you will be in a position to avoid conflicts and constant fights with people. When you are not conflicting with people, be sure they will give you the respect that you deserve. Being receptive to specific situations will show the kind of character you are. It does not matter whether you are at fault or not, avoid getting into fights, and people will treat you with respect.

When you know that you are unique from the other person, and you have differences, you will embrace diversity. When you appreciate diversity, you will have a chance to explore all the possibilities that are there to lead you to success. When you understand the difference, you will attract respect from people from the diversified groups since they will feel part of you. You will have great ideas because of the many creative minds that you have brought together. The more brilliant ideas there is the likely hood that you will succeed in your missions. When you understand what your likes and dislikes are, you can make decisions based on what you prefer. When you do something out of a will, you will have good results compared to what you are being forced. You will put all the senses at work so that they can gather the collect information for you. That is when you are going to make choices based on your instincts, and that will not mislead you. You will make implementations on the decisions and you will end up being successful.

When you know your personality type, you will be in a position to see the field in which you can do better. You will know the responsibilities that you can handle thoroughly and the goals you can achieve in a given time. Understanding your personality will help you in finding out the career that fits your best. That is where you ought to invest your energy as well as resources to be successful.

CONCLUSION

At this point, I hope you have gotten a keen insight into the world of body language and all of the aspects that pertain to reading people and techniques to analyze them. Now I would like to recommend you the first volume of the series (Dark Psychology Secrets) to learn what are mental manipulation, persuasion techniques, and mind control methods.

So, what's next?

I would greatly encourage you to take the knowledge you have learned in this book and put it to good use. The techniques outlined in this book are intended to help you get the most out of your own talents and abilities by removing barriers which often keep well-intended folks from getting ahead in life.

Ultimately, it is up to you to decide how you will use this information in your own life. So, do take the time to go over any of the tips, strategies, techniques and concepts contained in this book. By going over the information in this book, you will be able to better fixate the knowledge in your mind.

Also, if you have found this book to useful and informative, do tell your friends, family and colleagues about it. I would greatly appreciate a positive recommendation from my readers.

See you next time.